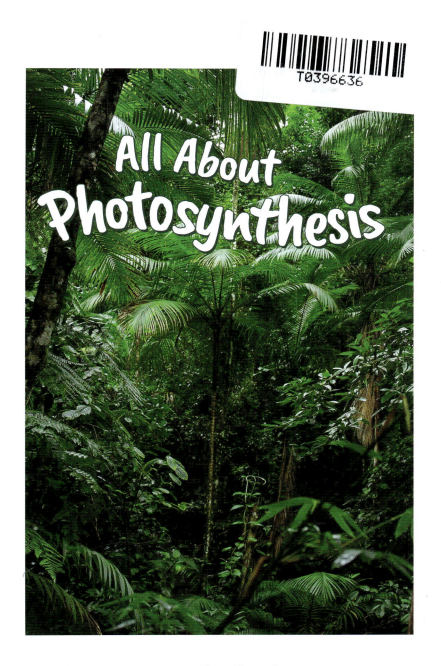

All About Photosynthesis

Monika Davies

Consultants

Matthew Fleming
Horticulturalist
Smithsonian Gardens

Cheryl Lane, M.Ed.
Seventh Grade Science Teacher
Chino Valley Unified School District

Michelle Wertman, M.S.Ed.
Literacy Specialist
New York City Public Schools

Publishing Credits

Rachelle Cracchiolo, M.S.Ed., *Publisher*
Emily R. Smith, M.A.Ed., *SVP of Content Development*
Véronique Bos, *VP of Creative*
Dani Neiley, *Editor*
Robin Erickson, *Senior Art Director*
Jill Malcolm, *Senior Graphic Designer*

Smithsonian Enterprises

Avery Naughton, *Licensing Coordinator*
Paige Towler, *Editorial Lead*
Jill Corcoran, *Senior Director, Licensed Publishing*
Brigid Ferraro, *Vice President of New Business and Licensing*
Carol LeBlanc, *President*

Image Credits: p.25 (top) Alamy; p.26 Getty Images;
all other images from iStock and/or Shutterstock.

Library of Congress Cataloging in Publication Control Number: 2024024232

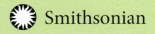

© 2025 Smithsonian Institution. The name "Smithsonian" and the Smithsonian logo are registered trademarks owned by the Smithsonian Institution.

This book may not be reproduced or distributed in any way without prior written consent from the publisher.

5482 Argosy Avenue
Huntington Beach, CA 92649
www.tcmpub.com
ISBN 979-8-7659-6860-4
© 2025 Teacher Created Materials, Inc.
Printed by: 51497
Printed in : China

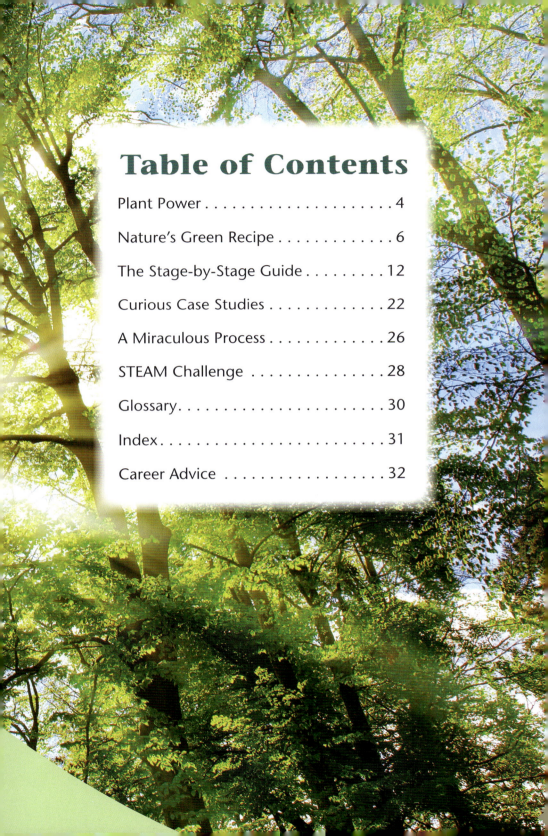

Table of Contents

Plant Power 4

Nature's Green Recipe 6

The Stage-by-Stage Guide 12

Curious Case Studies 22

A Miraculous Process 26

STEAM Challenge 28

Glossary. 30

Index. 31

Career Advice 32

Plant Power

Earth is a safe and comfortable home for countless living things, including humans. There are many reasons why Earth is the only known planet that can host life. For instance, the world gets an ideal amount of light and warmth from the sun. There is also enough liquid water to sustain life across the globe. And Earth is home to organisms called *autotrophs*. There are many kinds of autotrophs, but the best-known are plants with green leaves. These organisms use a process called *photosynthesis* to make their own food. This process also ensures that Earth can support life.

Whether they grow in nature or in small pots inside, all plants perform photosynthesis.

Photosynthesis allows plants to sustain themselves as they transform from sprouts into fully grown plants.

Photosynthesis roughly translates from Greek to "putting together with light." That's because one crucial **reactant** of this process is sunlight. This chemical reaction has many complex steps. But it only requires a few key reactants—carbon dioxide, water, and sunlight—to work.

The process of photosynthesis creates two products: oxygen and **glucose**. Both are necessary for life on Earth. Oxygen allows humans and animals to breathe, while glucose provides energy for all living things. Without photosynthesis, life on Earth would not exist. Let's break down how this process works and consider the power of plants on Earth.

Nature's Green Recipe

Just like humans, plants need food to survive. However, unlike humans, plants can't walk into a grocery store to buy ingredients for their next meal. They also can't eat a meal at a restaurant or order food for delivery. Instead, plants have to make food themselves.

Photosynthesis is a process that changes energy from the sun into chemical energy. Three **essential** reactants, or ingredients, are needed for plants to make their meals. Let's examine the recipe and how these ingredients are gathered.

Ingredient #1: Carbon Dioxide

Every day, humans breathe in a gas called *oxygen.* Then, they breathe out a gas called *carbon dioxide.* Humans must do this to stay alive. Just like humans, plants also need these gases to survive. But plants have different **respiratory** needs than humans. Plants take in carbon dioxide and let out oxygen.

Carbon dioxide is the first ingredient in the photosynthesis recipe. It is a greenhouse gas that has quite a reputation! Most people know it as a heat-trapping gas. This gas exists in Earth's atmosphere, keeping the planet at a comfortable temperature for living things. Some natural events can lead to a release of carbon dioxide. For instance, this gas is released when a volcano erupts. But it is released when people **extract** or burn fossil fuels, too.

SCIENCE

Climate Change

The amount of carbon dioxide in Earth's atmosphere is rapidly rising. This is leading to rising global temperatures. Higher temperatures can have negative effects on weather patterns and life on the planet.

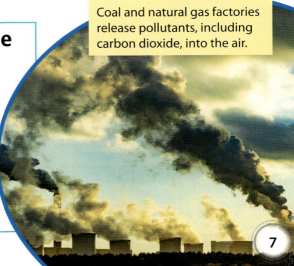

Coal and natural gas factories release pollutants, including carbon dioxide, into the air.

Autotrophs take in carbon dioxide through their stomata. Stomata are tiny pores that exist on different parts of a plant. Stomata are round and have holes in their centers, making them look like tiny bagels. Gases, including carbon dioxide, can move in or out of a plant through stomata.

Stomata are usually found on the bottom side of a plant's leaves. This location protects them from the intense glare of the sun or kicked-up dust. However, stomata can be found in other places, too. Depending on the plant, stomata can be found on the top side of leaves, flower petals, stems, or even on roots.

stomata

Banyan trees have unique roots that sprout from branches and grow down into the ground.

Ingredient #2: Water

Just like humans, autotrophs require water to survive and thrive. Water helps move **nutrients** throughout plants to help them grow and reproduce. This clear, odorless liquid is the second ingredient needed for photosynthesis. While some autotrophs have access to an endless supply of water, others do not. In certain environments, such as deserts, plants have special adaptations that allow them to get enough water. They may store it in their stems for later use.

Most plants draw in water through their root systems. Many plants have short, prickly roots that are fringed with thousands of little hairs. These hairs expand the surface area of their root systems, giving them the best chance to take in water.

Roots need adequate soil to grow.

Ingredient #3: Sunlight

Sunlight, or light energy, illuminates Earth. It can transform into heat as it hits a surface, creating warmth. And light energy is what powers up the process of photosynthesis. It is the final ingredient in the recipe.

Plant cells contain a key **organelle** that interacts with light energy. It is called a *chloroplast*. Animal and human cells do not have this type of organelle. It is only necessary for photosynthesis, so plants are the only organisms that have it. Chloroplasts contain a green **pigment** known as chlorophyll. Both chloroplasts and chlorophyll are found in the green tissue cells of plant leaves.

Desert plants, like these saguaro cacti, receive a large amount of sunlight.

Chlorophyll absorbs and stores light energy. It acts like a sponge, soaking up and holding light. This energy fuels the process of photosynthesis. Chlorophyll is also the reason why plants are green. When white light hits a plant, chlorophyll soaks up energy from blue and red wavelengths. But it does not absorb green light. Instead, the pigment reflects the emerald-tinted waves.

The recipe to start the process of photosynthesis is straightforward. Plants need only three ingredients: carbon dioxide, water, and sunlight. Once they have these, they're ready to start!

Under a microscope, tiny green chloroplasts become visible.

FUN FACT

Even on a cloudy day, most plants can make food. That's because clouds typically don't block all the sunlight. Some light still filters through the sky to Earth's surface. That means plants won't go hungry when the weather is bad.

The Stage-by-Stage Guide

From start to finish, cooking up a **nutritious** meal requires many steps. Likewise, photosynthesis is a multi-stage process. But instead of using pots and pans on a stove, autotrophs work with a series of chemical reactions. All these reactions occur inside plants, hidden from the human eye.

Pre-Stage: Reactants

Photosynthesis can only start once an autotroph has all the reactants: carbon dioxide, water, and sunlight. On the surface, this recipe may seem simple. But it is rigid and cannot handle substitutions like human recipes can. If one reactant is missing or there is not enough of it, photosynthesis will not occur. When all reactants are in place, an autotroph can start making its own food.

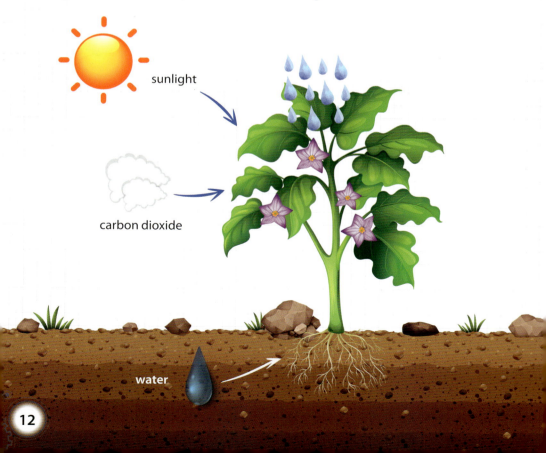

Stage 1: Light-Dependent Reactions

The first stage of photosynthesis involves a set of light-dependent reactions. To kick off this part of the process, a steady stream of sunlight is needed. During this stage, light energy starts to **convert**, or change, to chemical energy.

For most plants, this stage takes place in a specific part of the plant. Many plants conduct photosynthesis in the middle layer of their leaf tissue. This layer is known as *mesophyll*, and it is often the main hub for photosynthesis. Have you ever seen a plant's leaves stretching toward the sun? They do that to get as much sunlight onto their leaves as they can.

TECHNOLOGY

Artificial Photosynthesis

Humans have tried to create technology that mimics photosynthesis. The closest we have come is with photovoltaic technology. This involves using solar cells that change sunlight into electricity. But it is not as efficient as photosynthesis. For now, plants still hold the secret to effectively converting the sun's energy!

At first glance, mesophyll tissue contains many cells. These cells are packed full of chloroplasts. Inside each chloroplast are stacks of thylakoids. These are flattened sacs that contain chlorophyll, the green pigment that soaks up sunlight like a sponge. Together, the stacks make up the inner thylakoid **membrane**. This key membrane is where light-dependent reactions occur.

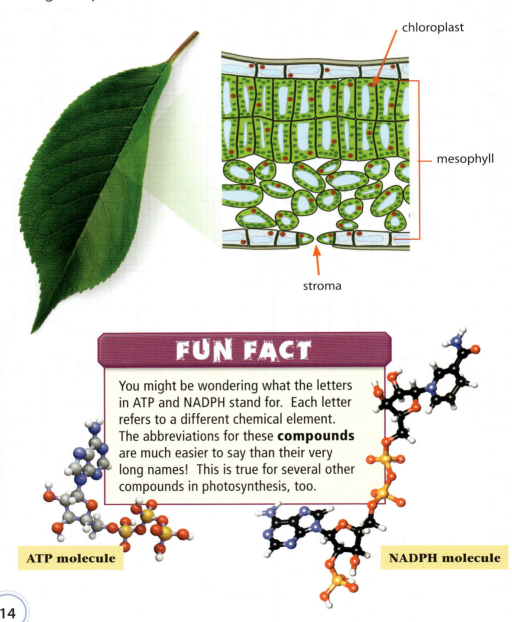

FUN FACT

You might be wondering what the letters in ATP and NADPH stand for. Each letter refers to a different chemical element. The abbreviations for these **compounds** are much easier to say than their very long names! This is true for several other compounds in photosynthesis, too.

ATP molecule

NADPH molecule

Light-Dependent Reactions

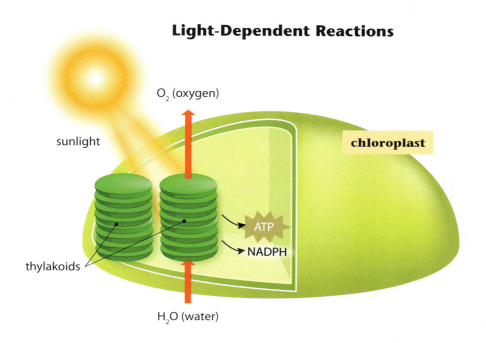

Here's a closer look at these reactions. As sunlight shines on a plant, chlorophyll captures the light energy. A **photon** of light hits and energetically excites a chlorophyll **molecule**. In turn, this triggers a process that divides a nearby water molecule. (This is why water is a vital reactant for photosynthesis!) As the water molecule divides, an oxygen **atom** is released. That atom then bonds with another oxygen atom. As a result, a complete oxygen molecule is formed. Plants release this oxygen, and it becomes part of the air humans breathe. Thanks to this part of photosynthesis, living beings around the planet breathe in fresh oxygen.

At this stage, two more compounds are produced. They are called *ATP* and *NADPH*. ATP is a molecule that can store energy. NADPH is an **electron carrier**. Both compounds are necessary for the second stage of photosynthesis.

Once oxygen, ATP, and NADPH are created, the first stage of photosynthesis is complete. And this marks the halfway point of the process.

Stage 2: Light-Independent Reactions

The second stage of photosynthesis involves light-independent reactions. Some scientists refer to these as dark reactions because they do not need steady sunlight. So, this part of photosynthesis can take place during the day or night. These reactions take place in the stroma. Stroma is a fluid that fills spaces within chloroplasts.

The energy from the first stage of photosynthesis kicks off what is known as the Calvin cycle. This cycle is crucial for food production. It is how plants make glucose, a type of **carbohydrate**. There are four steps in this cycle.

Light-Independent Reactions

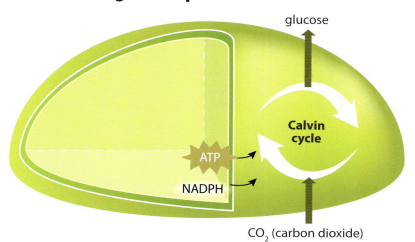

Step 1: Carbon Fixation

The first step of the Calvin cycle is called *carbon fixation*. This is where carbon dioxide comes into play. First, carbon dioxide enters the stroma. Every carbon atom in each carbon dioxide molecule shares the same goal: find a friend. Each carbon atom pairs with another carbon molecule inside the stroma. The molecule they pair with is called *RuBP*. When these two find each other, they bond and become a compound. An **enzyme** called *rubisco* holds them together. Think of it like a crispy rice treat: the cereal is the carbon, and the sticky marshmallow is the rubisco.

This new compound does not stay together for long. Just like a crispy rice treat, it can be cut in half. Once it forms, the compound divides quickly and neatly into two molecules. These two molecules are known as 3-PGA compounds. The *3* refers to the number of carbon atoms in each molecule. These compounds transform in the next step of the Calvin cycle.

Step 2: Reduction

Step two of the Calvin cycle is known as reduction. This is where the ATP and NADPH from the previous stage now lend a helping hand. Both compounds are used to reduce the two 3-PGA compounds.

At this step, the 3-PGA compounds transform into two sugar molecules. These molecules are called *G3P* for short. ATP gives the energy to power this transformative reaction. And NADPH helps, too. Each compound donates **electrons** to help make G3P.

This step creates the building blocks that are needed to make glucose. These G3P molecules are the cornerstones of plant food.

MATHEMATICS

The Basic Formula

Photosynthesis uses different elements. These elements can be shown in a chemical equation. To start, six carbon molecules (CO_2) and six water molecules (H_2O) are needed. When light energy is added, one glucose molecule ($C_6H_{12}O_6$) and six oxygen molecules (O_2) are made.

$$6CO_2 + 6H_2O \xrightarrow{\text{light energy}} C_6H_{12}O_6 + 6O_2$$

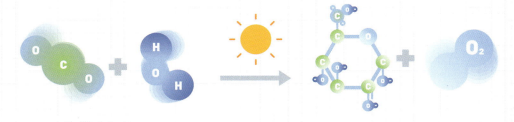

6x Carbon Dioxide CO_2 + 6x Water H_2O → Light energy → Glucose $C_6H_{12}O_6$ + 6x Oxygen O_2

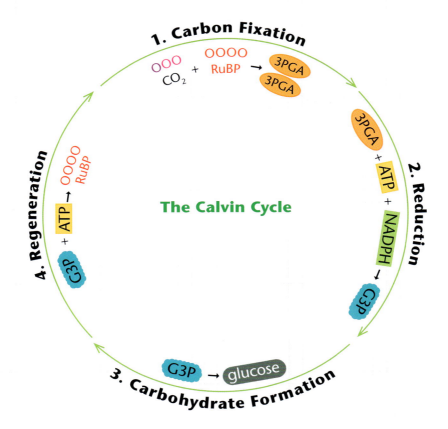

Step 3: Carbohydrate Formation

The third step of the Calvin cycle is carbohydrate formation. This is when some G3P molecules transform into glucose. Some scientists argue that this is the most critical step. That's because the Calvin cycle's ultimate purpose is to make glucose.

Step 4: Regeneration

In the fourth step, the Calvin cycle comes full circle. At this point, the remaining G3P molecules go through another series of reactions. Energy from ATP is needed for these reactions. During this step, the G3P molecules change into RuBP molecules. These are the molecules seen in the first step of the Calvin cycle! With the creation of RuBP, the cycle starts over. These molecules wait to receive carbon from carbon dioxide molecules.

Post-Stage: Feast of Sugar

There are two final products of photosynthesis. Oxygen is one of them. And for an autotroph, the most crucial product is glucose. Glucose is a simple carbohydrate, and it is the food that sustains autotrophs. Glucose has different purposes. For instance, it can link up to build complex carbohydrates. One example is cellulose, which is used to build cell walls. Glucose can also convert into different types of sugars. Examples include fructose and sucrose. These sugars can be found in fruits and vegetables.

The Flow of Energy

Photosynthesis is a unique process that has countless benefits for all living things. It transforms light energy into chemical energy, which exists in the form of carbohydrates. This is how plants receive the energy they need to grow. And that's why plants are known as producers! They are able to produce, or make, their own food.

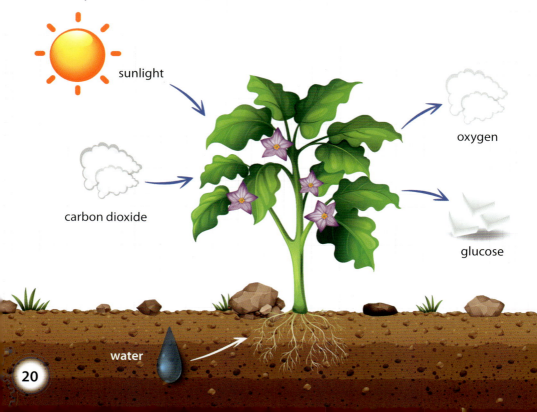

But the energy plants create does not stop there. Just like plants, humans and animals also gain energy from carbohydrates. These consumers can eat plants and all the nutrients they contain. Fruits and vegetables help fuel the bodies of humans and animals. Every living being gets fuel from carbohydrates.

FUN FACT

Plants thrive on feasts of sugar. But humans need to be careful with their sugar consumption. Added sugar can be found in candy, soft drinks, cookies, and other sweet treats. Eating too much of this type of sugar can lead to an increase in calories, which can lead to weight gain. It can also lead to increased blood pressure, creating a higher risk of heart disease.

Curious Case Studies

Photosynthesis is a crucial process on the planet. Without it, autotrophs would not survive. However, plants around the world have different access to resources. Some plants bake in the sun and lack a consistent supply of water. Others soak up rain every day and can barely catch a ray of light. In response, these plants—and one animal!—have found unique ways to make their own food.

Desert Plants

Most deserts get around 25 centimeters (10 inches) of rain every year. Compared to other environments, this is a very small amount. Even though deserts are dry environments, plants can still grow there. Green, prickly cacti are a common sight in deserts. These plants rarely have access to water, a crucial reactant for photosynthesis. So, they have adapted to this lack of water by having a unique approach to this process.

Cacti use CAM photosynthesis to make their food. It works differently from regular photosynthesis. During CAM photosynthesis, cacti only open their stomata under night skies. This useful strategy allows them to survive in their harsh environment. Cacti take in carbon dioxide at night when the air is cooler. At cooler temperatures, plants lose less water. This helps cacti retain more water. Cacti also have thick, waxy stems that help them store water. Their built-in storage helps them survive long periods of time without a single drop of rain.

bunny ears cacti

Beneath the spines of saguaro cacti are layers of sponge-like tissue that store water.

ENGINEERING

Living on Less Water

CAM photosynthesis allows cacti to survive on very little water. Some scientists want to re-create this process in other plants to make them more **drought** resistant. These scientists are working on ways to engineer corn and wheat crops to use CAM photosynthesis. It's still a work in progress, though!

Rainforest Plants

Rainforests are famous for their moist surroundings. However, plants that live in a rainforest's **understory** only catch moments of speckled sunlight. The plants that grow in this dark area only get about one to five percent of the sun that beams down. Since sunshine is scarce, these plants have adapted their appearances.

Rainforest plants often have unusual leaves. Their wide leaves grow horizontally to soak up as much sun as possible. These leaves often grow at different angles to widen their sun-catching surface areas. Many leaves end with angled tips, allowing water to run off quickly. This helps the leaves absorb more sunlight. It also stops fungi and moss from growing on the surface of the leaves, which would block sunlight.

Monstera plants have holes in their leaves, allowing them to spread over a wider area and access more sunlight.

Thousands of different plant species live in rainforests around the world.

Emerald-Green Sea Slugs

Most autotrophs are plants with green leaves. But one tiny animal has found a way to use photosynthesis. *Elysia chlorotica* is also known as the emerald-green sea slug. These sea slugs are a vibrant green color, thanks to their meals of algae. When they eat algae, they absorb the chloroplasts inside. This allows them to undergo photosynthesis while sunbathing! Scientists have also discovered that these little animals can go months without a single bite to eat. These sea slugs are a rare find, though. Many mysteries still surround how these little animals use photosynthesis.

The green color from chloroplasts allows these sea slugs to blend in with the seafloor and avoid predators.

Green algae is a food source for emerald-green sea slugs.

A Miraculous Process

On the surface, photosynthesis can seem like a straightforward process. After all, a plant needs only carbon dioxide, water, and some sunlight! But it involves a multi-stage transformation. The process starts when light energy enters a plant. After many complex reactions, a treasure trove of chemical energy is created.

Some people refer to this process as "nature's miracle." Indeed, scientists have puzzled over it for decades. Thanks to advances in technology, there is an increased understanding of this unique process. However, humans still struggle to replicate its results. Solar technology involves some aspects of photosynthesis. But to date, there is no energy match for how plants make their food.

Photosynthesis is an invisible process to humans. But the impact of it is felt in every part of people's lives. Photosynthesis helps color our world with shades of green. It provides us with food that fuels us. It also gives us some of the oxygen that fills our lungs. Without photosynthesis, life would not exist on our planet. This process is a natural marvel, worthy of recognition and understanding.

ARTS

Plant Art

Before photography existed, people would draw plants so they could study them. A British artist named Sarah Drake became an expert in plant illustration. She mostly painted orchids, and she illustrated several books. A group of 10 different orchid species is named after her! It is called *Drakaea*.

STEAM CHALLENGE

Define the Problem

Agriculture, the science and practice of farming, is an important industry all around the world. Engineers design greenhouses so that farmers can grow different plants in controlled environments. Your task is to design and build a model greenhouse. Your greenhouse must allow sunlight to come through, include an entry point to water the plants inside, and have enough space to house three clay pots.

Constraints: You may only use the materials provided to you. You must meet the three conditions for plants to grow.

Criteria: Your model must open and close to allow for watering. It has to allow sunlight to come through the interior. Your greenhouse must fit three small clay pots inside.

Research and Brainstorm

What do plants need to survive and thrive? Why do farmers use greenhouses to grow produce? What are key elements of greenhouse design?

Design and Build

Sketch two or more designs for your greenhouse. Label the parts and the materials. Choose the design you think will work best. Then, build your greenhouse.

Test and Improve

Share your greenhouse model with others. Demonstrate how it works by opening it up to place the three small clay pots inside. Explain key features of the greenhouse and why your team chose these materials. What can you add or change to make your model more efficient? Modify your design and rebuild it as needed. Reassess how well it meets the criteria.

Reflect and Share

Which types of materials could you use to build a larger model of your greenhouse? How could you test your model? What part of this challenge are you most proud of?

Glossary

atom—the smallest part of an element that can exist either by itself or in a combination

carbohydrate—a chemical substance made up of carbon, hydrogen, and oxygen that provides energy

compounds—substances created when the atoms of two or more chemical elements combine

convert—to change something into a different form or use

drought—a long period of dry weather

electron carrier—a molecule that can take in electrons from another molecule and then take those electrons to another molecule

electrons—negatively charged particles that are found in atoms

enzyme—a special protein produced by a cell that starts or speeds up a chemical reaction

essential—incredibly important and necessary

extract—to get a substance from something using a machine or chemicals

glucose—a type of sugar that occurs widely in nature

membrane—a thin barrier layer of an organism's body part, such as a cell, tissue, or organ

molecule—a group of atoms bonded together as the smallest possible unit of a chemical compound

nutrients—substances that organisms need to live and grow

nutritious—having elements that an organism needs to be healthy and grow

organelle—a specialized part of a cell that is located in the cytoplasm

photon—a tiny particle of electromagnetic radiation, such as light

pigment—a natural material or substance that gives color

reactant—a substance that takes part in and undergoes change during a chemical reaction

respiratory—relating to breathing

understory—a layer of plants that is above the forest floor, growing under the top layer of a forest

Index

3-PGA, 17–18
ATP, 14–15, 18–19
cacti, 5, 10, 22–23
Calvin cycle, 16–19
CAM photosynthesis, 22–23
carbohydrate formation, 19
carbon dioxide, 5, 7–8, 11–12, 17–20, 22, 26
carbon fixation, 17, 19
cellulose, 20
chlorophyll, 10–11, 14–15
chloroplasts, 10–11, 14, 16, 25
emerald-green sea slug, 25
fructose, 20
G3P, 18–19
glucose, 5, 16–20

light-dependent reactions, 13–15
light-independent reactions, 16–17
mesophyll, 13–14
NADPH, 14–15, 17–19
oxygen, 5, 7, 15, 18, 20, 26
rainforest plants, 24
reduction, 18–19
regeneration, 19
RuBP, 17, 19
stomata, 8, 22
stroma, 14, 16–17
sucrose, 20
thylakoid membrane, 14

tropical plants in Costa Rica

CAREER ADVICE
from Smithsonian

Do you dream of working with plants?
Here are some tips to keep in mind for the future.

"Get involved in local gardening clubs or start one at your school. There are many different disciplines of horticulture, such as plant propagation, greenhouse management, caring for specialized types of plants, and maintaining interior plant displays. Don't limit yourself to just one! Explore as much as you can!"

– *Joe Curley, Horticulturist, Smithsonian Gardens*

"I encourage you to learn more about one of Earth's most significant flowering plant families. For example, every orchid has a unique story that can inspire us to study its intricate relationships with other living things, from microscopic fungi to fluttery butterflies. Orchids are indicators of the health of an ecosystem. If orchids are thriving, it is a sign that our planet's ecosystems are also thriving."

– *Justin Kondrat, Horticulturist, Smithsonian Gardens*